Fact Finders®

CAUSE AND EFFECT

MR. Madison's WAR

CAUSES AND EFFECTS

of the War of 1812

BY KASSANDRA RADOMSKI

Consultant:
Keith A. Herkalo, President
Battle of Plattsburgh Association
Plattsburgh, New York

CAPSTONE PRESS
a capstone imprint

Fact Finders Books are published by Capstone Press,
1710 Roe Crest Drive, North Mankato, Minnesota 56003
www.capstonepub.com

Library of Congress Cataloging-in-Publication Data
Radomski, Kassandra.
  Mr. Madison's war : causes and effects of the War of 1812 / by Kassandra Radomski.
p. cm.—(Fact finders. Cause and effect)
Includes bibliographical references and index.
Summary: "Describes the causes of the War of 1812 and its effects on U.S. history"
—Provided by publisher.
ISBN 978-1-4765-0239-7 (library binding)—ISBN 978-1-4765-3405-3 (pbk.)—
ISBN 978-1-4765-3413-8 (ebook pdf)
1. United States—History—War of 1812—Causes—Juvenile literature. 2. United
States—History—War of 1812—Influence—Juvenile literature. I. Title. II. Title: Mister
Madison's war.
E354.R34 2014
973.5'2—dc23   2013007026

Editorial Credits
Erika L. Shores, editor; Alison Thiele, designer; Svetlana Zhurkin, media researcher;
    Laura Manthe, production specialist

Photo Credits
Corbis: Bettmann, 24, Stapleton Collection, 9; Courtesy Scotts Bluff National
Monument, 23; CriaImages: Jay Robert Nash Collection, 7; Library of Congress, cover,
4, 5, 11, 12, 13, 14, 17, 18–19, 21, 27; Newscom: Picture History, 20; Shutterstock: Frank
L. Junior, 28, spirit of america, 15

Printed in the United States of America in Stevens Point, Wisconsin
052014   008277R

Table OF CONTENTS

Road to War

From 1775 to 1783, Americans fought for their independence from Great Britain. When they won the Revolutionary War, Americans were finally free of British rule and interference. Or so they thought.

After the war the relationship between the United States and Great Britain remained tense. Less than 30 years later, the two countries would again be at war.

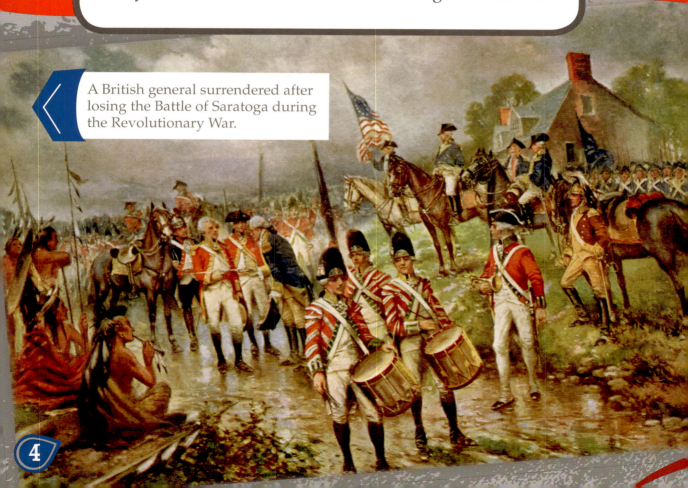

A British general surrendered after losing the Battle of Saratoga during the Revolutionary War.

The Battle of Lake Erie was an important victory for the United States during the War of 1812.

The War of 1812 (1812–1815) didn't last as long as the Revolutionary War. It didn't have as great of an impact on the country either. But it did affect how the U.S. government was run. It also affected where Americans lived and their relationship with American Indians. What issues and conflicts led the United States and Great Britain back to war?

What Caused THE WAR OF 1812?

Several factors led the United States into war against Great Britain for the second time.

Cause #1—American Sailors Forced into British Service

On June 22, 1807, the USS *Chesapeake* set sail off the Virginia coast. Suddenly the crew noticed that a British ship was chasing the *Chesapeake*. The other ship, the HMS *Leopard*, forced the *Chesapeake* to stop. The *Leopard's* captain, Salisbury Humphreys, demanded to come aboard the *Chesapeake*. U.S. Commander James Barron refused. The British began firing at the *Chesapeake*. The American crew fired one gun and scrambled to get off the ship. Eighteen men were injured. Three were killed. The British took four men off the *Chesapeake* and forced them to work on the *Leopard*.

Forced to surrender, James Barron offered his sword to Salisbury Humphreys.

The act of taking U.S. sailors off their ships and forcing them to work for Great Britain was called **impressment**. The British had been impressing sailors for several years before what became known as the *Chesapeake-Leopard* Affair. Americans were furious about this practice and wanted it to stop.

impressment: the act of forcing someone into military service

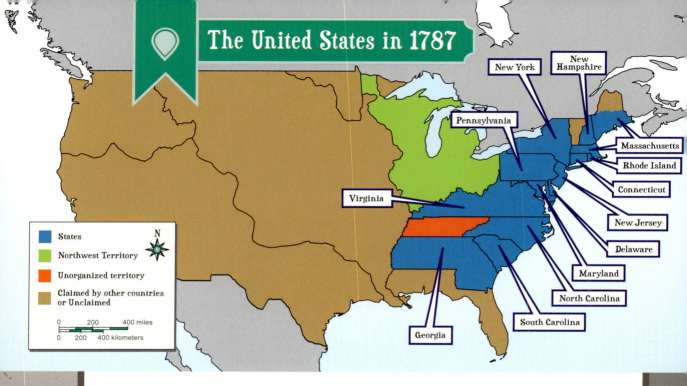

The United States in 1787

New York
New Hampshire
Pennsylvania
Massachusetts
Rhode Island
Connecticut
New Jersey
Delaware
Virginia
Maryland
North Carolina
South Carolina
Georgia

States
Northwest Territory
Unorganized territory
Claimed by other countries or Unclaimed

N

0   200   400 miles
0   200   400 kilometers

Cause #2—U.S. Expansion

In the late 1700s the United States' territory spread from the Atlantic Ocean west to the Mississippi River. But the country was eager to expand even farther west. The United States also had its eye on British-controlled Canadian territories to the north. This situation worried the British government.

American Indians were also concerned. As white settlers moved west, they built farms and towns on land that the Indians used for hunting and trapping. The Indians didn't want settlers taking over more of their land. Indian leaders had to choose between being loyal to the United States or siding with the British. The Indians believed the British would be more likely to let them keep their land.

Cause #3—Trade Issues

By the early 1800s the United States was still a young, growing country. It made money and brought in needed supplies by trading **goods** with other countries. These goods were transported by ship. But the U.S. shipping trade was caught in the middle of sea battles between Great Britain and France. The two countries were fighting for control of trade on the Atlantic Ocean and for land.

France and Great Britain would block ships from reaching the other country's **ports**. This action created major hardships for the United States. Americans couldn't make money by selling goods to France. Great Britain also caused trouble by stealing goods from American ships. The U.S. government realized that this situation couldn't continue.

French and British ships fought each other in the Battle of Basque Roads in 1809.

goods: items that are bought and sold

port: a harbor or place where ships and boats can dock safely

THE United States AT WAR

President Thomas Jefferson tried to find peaceful solutions to the problems with Great Britain. After the *Chesapeake-Leopard* Affair, Jefferson asked Congress to pass the **Embargo** Act. This act prevented any ships from entering or leaving U.S. ports. It shut down U.S. trade. Jefferson thought the embargo would help the United States remain **neutral** in the war between France and Britain. But the act hurt the U.S. economy. The unpopular act lasted just 14 months.

When James Madison became president in 1809, he also tried to avoid war. Like Jefferson, Madison stopped the United States from trading with Great Britain and France. But Madison allowed the United States to keep trading with other countries. This didn't work either. Great Britain continued to stop U.S. ships, steal their goods, and impress American sailors.

embargo: an official order forbidding something from happening
neutral: not taking sides

Thomas Jefferson

Battle of Tippecanoe

A battle between American soldiers and American Indians finally led the United States to war with Great Britain. On November 7, 1811, the Battle of Tippecanoe was fought near an Indian village called Prophetstown in northern Indiana.

A Shawnee tribal leader named Tecumseh fought against white settlers moving into Indian lands. Tecumseh spent the summer and fall of 1811 traveling and spreading his message to other tribes. Before Tecumseh left, he warned his brother, Tenskwatawa, to avoid battle with the whites.

William Henry Harrison was the governor of Indiana Territory. He was worried about Tecumseh uniting the Indians against white settlers. On November 6 Harrison and about 1,000 troops set up camp near the village. Their plan was to attack Prophetstown the next morning.

Tenskwatawa knew the Americans were close by. He ignored his brother's warning and led an attack on the sleeping American soldiers. After two hours of fierce fighting, 62 American soldiers and about 50 American Indians were dead.

The two sides fought each other in the forests near Prophetstown.

War Hawks

A group of young congressmen blamed Great Britain for the Battle of Tippecanoe. They believed the British encouraged the Indians to attack the U.S. soldiers. These congressmen were called the War Hawks. They worked to convince President Madison that war was the best solution to the conflict with Britain.

Madison listened to the War Hawks. On June 1, 1812, he presented Congress with a list of complaints against Great Britain. Madison was angry at Britain for impressing sailors and interfering with trade. He also blamed Britain for worsening the United States' relationship with American Indians. On June 18, 1812, Congress declared war on Great Britain.

James Madison >

FAST FACT: Members of the Federalist political party opposed the War Hawks. Federalists were angry with President Madison for listening to the War Hawks. They called the War of 1812 "Mr. Madison's War."

Early Battles

In July 1812 more than 600 British and Canadian soldiers and American Indians surrounded U.S. Fort Mackinac. The fort was on Mackinac Island in Michigan Territory. Lieutenant Porter Hanks, the head of Fort Mackinac, was shocked. He hadn't been told the United States was at war! Without any shots fired, Hanks surrendered. The United States lost an important path to Canada.

On August 15 U.S. soldiers and their family members **evacuated** Fort Dearborn in present-day Chicago. American Indians killed more than half of the people fleeing the fort. On August 16 U.S. General William Hull surrendered his army at Fort Detroit in Michigan Territory.

The war was not off to a good start for the United States. But the United States did have an important victory at sea. On August 19, 1812, the USS *Constitution* faced the British ship HMS *Guerriere* off the coast of Nova Scotia, Canada. After a half-hour battle, the *Guerriere* was destroyed. This victory gave Americans confidence about their chance of winning the war.

The USS *Constitution* defeated the HMS *Guerriere.*

evacuate: to leave an area during a time of danger

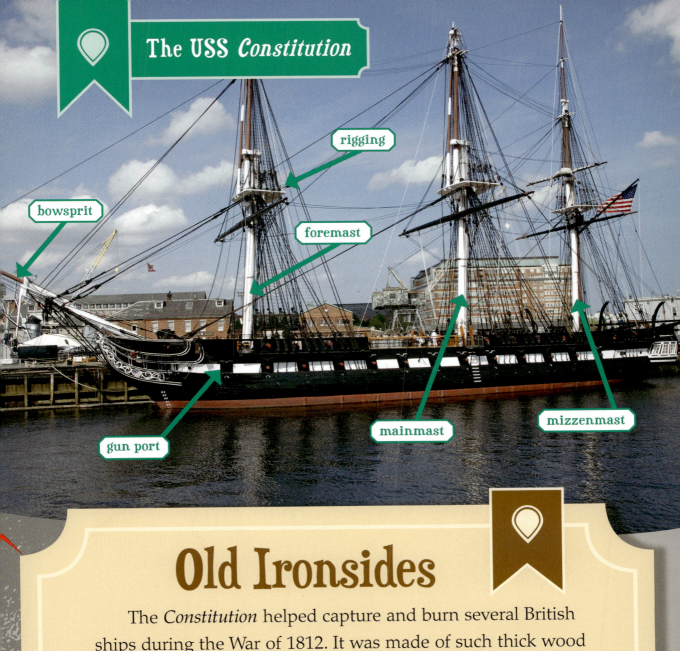

rigging

bowsprit

foremast

gun port

mainmast

mizzenmast

Old Ironsides

The *Constitution* helped capture and burn several British ships during the War of 1812. It was made of such thick wood that cannonballs often bounced right off it. One American sailor said, "Her sides are made of iron!" That's how it got its nickname, "Old Ironsides." The *Constitution* is now docked in Charlestown Navy Yard in Massachusetts as a museum ship.

Burning the Capitol

In May 1814 Great Britain won its war with France. With that war over, about 15,000 more British soldiers were available to fight the United States.

In mid-August, 4,500 British soldiers landed in Maryland. The U.S. Army realized the nation's capital was in danger. They gathered a force of about 6,000, mostly **militia**, on Bladensburg Road to fight 2,600 British troops on August 24. Despite having more troops, the Americans were defeated. The British soldiers continued their march to Washington, D.C.

When the British troops arrived in Washington, they set the U.S. Capitol on fire. Late in the evening British troops reached the president's house and set it on fire too.

Dolley Saves the Day

Residents of Washington, D.C., fled the city before the British soldiers. Before she left the president's house, later known as the White House, first lady Dolley Madison saved some important items. She wanted to take a portrait of George Washington, but the frame was screwed to the wall. She ordered the frame broken, and the portrait was removed and saved. Madison also grabbed a copy of the Declaration of Independence.

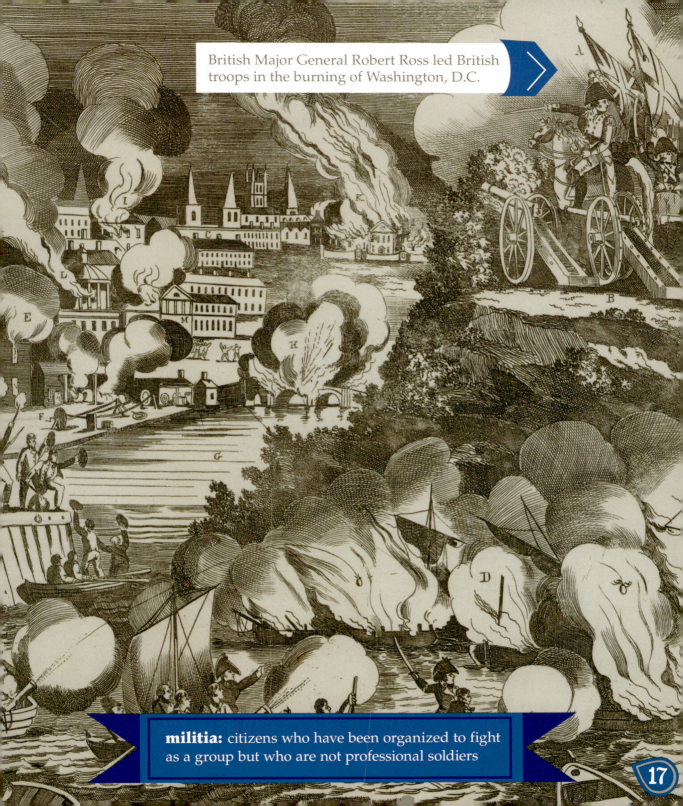

British Major General Robert Ross led British troops in the burning of Washington, D.C.

Key Victories

Two more important battles happened in the fall of 1814. On September 6 about 10,000 British troops reached Plattsburgh, New York, on the shores of Lake Champlain. Five days later a British fleet sailed to Plattsburgh. American naval and land forces awaited them. The two sides fired at each other for two hours and 20 minutes. In the end, the American forces won.

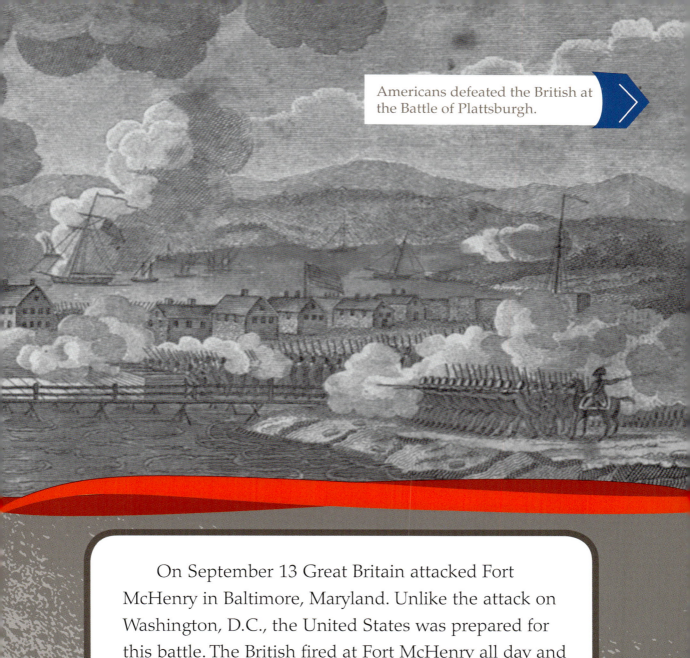

Americans defeated the British at the Battle of Plattsburgh.

On September 13 Great Britain attacked Fort McHenry in Baltimore, Maryland. Unlike the attack on Washington, D.C., the United States was prepared for this battle. The British fired at Fort McHenry all day and night. But the fort suffered little damage. There were few American deaths. The Americans had successfully defended the fort.

Peace Talks and Victory in New Orleans

In August 1814 American leaders including Henry Clay and John Quincy Adams traveled to Ghent, Belgium. There the Americans began peace talks with British officials. Finally, a peace **treaty** was signed on December 24, 1814. Word traveled slowly in those days, so few people knew.

Meanwhile the British sailed toward New Orleans. British Secretary of War Henry Bathurst believed attacking New Orleans would help force the United States to surrender. British troops attacked the city on January 8, 1815. General Andrew Jackson led the American troops. The battle lasted only about 30 minutes. In that time, 2,000 British soldiers and 71 American soldiers were injured or killed.

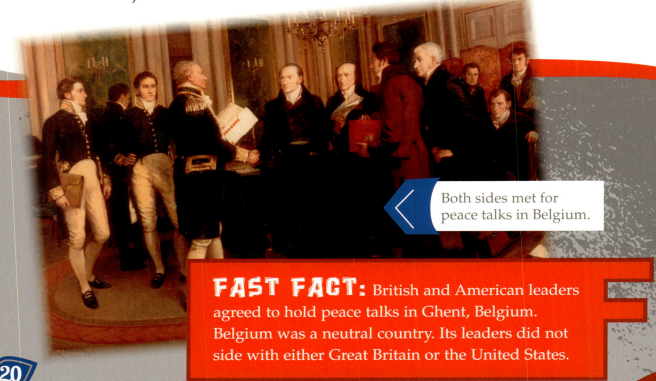

Both sides met for peace talks in Belgium.

FAST FACT: British and American leaders agreed to hold peace talks in Ghent, Belgium. Belgium was a neutral country. Its leaders did not side with either Great Britain or the United States.

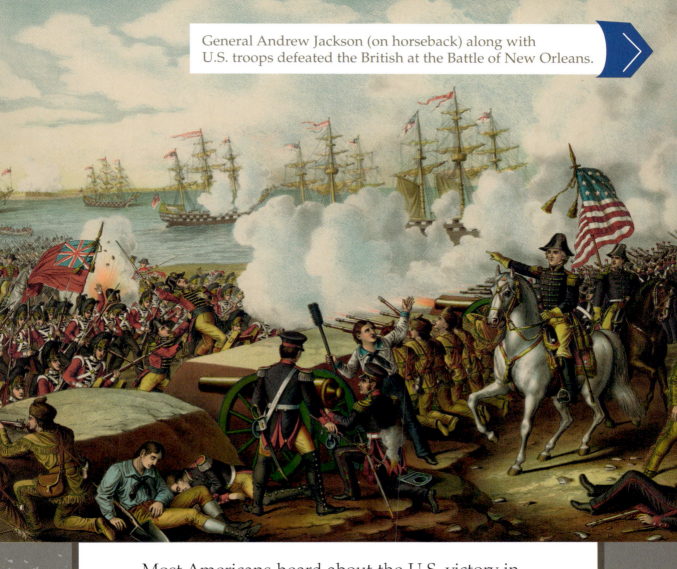

General Andrew Jackson (on horseback) along with U.S. troops defeated the British at the Battle of New Orleans.

Most Americans heard about the U.S. victory in New Orleans before learning about the peace treaty. They thought this victory was the reason for the end of the war.

treaty: an official agreement between two or more groups or countries

What Effects Did

THE WAR OF
1812 HAVE?

The British and the Americans celebrated the end of the war. Both had reasons to believe they had won. There were no clear winners in the War of 1812. But the war did cause some lasting effects in the young United States.

Effect #1—A Lost Way of Life

Although it wasn't clear what the United States and Great Britain gained from the War of 1812, there was one group that lost a great deal. This group was the American Indians.

The Treaty of Ghent said that American Indian rights and land would return to the way they were in 1811. But since Indian lands had no clear-cut **boundaries**, white Americans ignored this part of the treaty.

boundary: the line or border that separates one area from another

As settlers moved west, American Indians lost much of their lands. >

Americans stopped expanding into Indian territory in Canada. But they didn't stop taking over Indian territory in the United States. They pushed tribes off land they had lived on for hundreds of years. Along with their land, Indians were forced to give up their traditions and their way of life.

The Erie Canal opened shipping routes in the United States.

Effect #2—Continued Confidence

Because the United States successfully defended itself against Great Britain during the war, it gained the respect of other European countries. This boosted U.S. confidence and brought about a period called the "Era of Good Feelings." The confidence encouraged a spirit of growth in the United States that continued throughout the 1800s.

Effect #3—Economic Growth

The American economy grew stronger after the war. The disruptions in trade before and during the war forced the United States to build more factories. The country became less dependent on goods from other countries. For example, many cotton mills were built in the eastern United States to produce cloth. Before the war cotton cloth was brought in from Great Britain.

Transportation systems also expanded to send factory and mill products to other countries and U.S. regions. One of these systems was the Erie **Canal**. The canal connected the Atlantic Ocean to the Great Lakes in 1825.

canal: a channel dug across land to connect two bodies of water

Effect #4—The U.S. Political System

The Federalist and Democratic-Republican political parties were powerful during and after the Revolutionary War. The Federalist party strongly opposed the War of 1812. Federalists believed that a war against Great Britain wouldn't benefit the United States.

After the war many Americans believed that the Federalists weren't patriotic and didn't represent their needs. By 1816 the party had fallen apart because of lack of support. The breakdown of the Federalist party allowed the rise of the Democrat and Republican parties that we have in the United States today.

Effect #5—The National Anthem

"Oh, say can you see by the dawn's early light ..."
American lawyer Francis Scott Key wrote these familiar words after watching the British attack Fort McHenry. When Key awoke the morning after the battle he saw an enormous American flag still flying over Fort McHenry. Key was so moved by what he saw, he wrote a poem. His poem was set to music and called "The Star-Spangled Banner." In 1931 it became the national anthem.

Seeing the American flag wave over Fort McHenry inspired Francis Scott Key to write a poem.

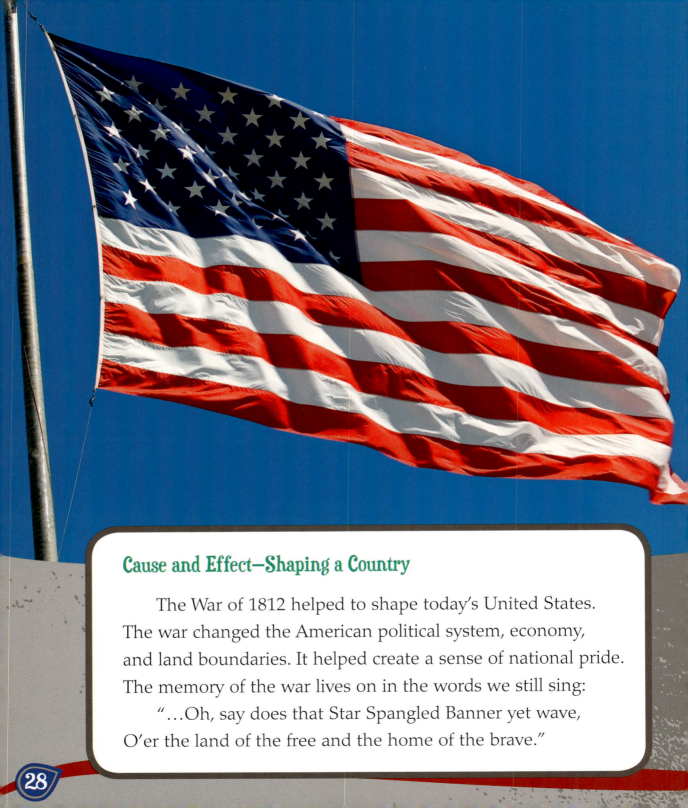

Cause and Effect—Shaping a Country

The War of 1812 helped to shape today's United States. The war changed the American political system, economy, and land boundaries. It helped create a sense of national pride. The memory of the war lives on in the words we still sing:

"...Oh, say does that Star Spangled Banner yet wave, O'er the land of the free and the home of the brave."

Timeline of Key Dates

1803-1812:
British impressment of American sailors

June 22, 1807:
USS *Chesapeake* stopped by HMS *Leopard*

December 22, 1807:
Embargo Act goes into effect.

November 7, 1811:
Battle of Tippecanoe

June 18, 1812:
The United States declares war on Great Britain.

July 1812:
The U.S. invasion of Canada begins.

July 17, 1812:
British forces capture Mackinac Island.

August 15, 1812:
The British win the Battle of Fort Dearborn.

August 16, 1812:
Great Britain captures Detroit.

August 19, 1812:
The USS *Constitution* defeats HMS *Guerriere*.

January 22, 1813:
Great Britain defeats the United States in the Battle of Frenchtown.

October 5, 1813:
The United States wins the Battle of the Thames.

August 24-25, 1814:
British troops occupy and burn Washington, D.C.

September 11, 1814:
The United States wins the Battles of Plattsburgh.

September 14, 1814:
The United States overcomes the British attack on Fort McHenry in Baltimore.

December 24, 1814:
The Treaty of Ghent ends the war.

January 8, 1815:
The United States defeats the British at the Battle of New Orleans.

GLOSSARY

boundary (BOUN-duh-ree)—the line or border that separates one area from another

canal (kuh-NAL)—a channel dug across land to connect two bodies of water

embargo (em-BAR-goh)—an official order forbidding something from happening, such as trade

evacuate (i-VA-kyuh-wayt)—to leave an area during a time of danger

goods (GUDZ)—items that can be bought or sold

impressment (im-PRESS-muhnt)—the act of forcing someone into military service

militia (muh-LISH-uh)—citizens who have been organized to fight as a group but who are not professional soldiers

neutral (NOO-truhl)—not taking sides

port (PORT)—a harbor or place where boats and ships can dock safely and load and unload goods

treaty (TREE-tee)—an official agreement between two or more groups or countries

READ MORE

Benn, Carl. *The War of 1812: The Fight for American Trade Rights.* Early American Wars. New York: Rosen Pub., 2011.

Flatt, Lizann. *The Legacy of the War of 1812.* Documenting the War of 1812. New York: Crabtree Pub. Co., 2012.

Isaacs, Sally Senzell. *What Caused the War of 1812?* Documenting the War of 1812. New York: Crabtree Pub. Co., 2011.

Kulling, Monica. *Francis Scott Key's Star-Spangled Banner.* Step into Reading. New York: Random House Children's Books, 2012.

INTERNET SITES

FactHound offers a safe, fun way to find Internet sites related to this book. All of the sites on FactHound have been researched by our staff.

Here's all you do:

Visit *www.facthound.com*

Type in this code: 9781476502397

Super-cool stuff! Check out projects, games and lots more at **www.capstonekids.com**

CRITICAL THINKING USING THE COMMON CORE

1. Many American Indians fought for Great Britain during the War of 1812. Why did they decide to fight on Britain's side? Support your answer with details from the text. (Key Ideas and Details)

2. The War Hawks and the Federalists had very different positions on going to war with Great Britain. Describe the reasoning behind each group's opinion, including how and why they differed. (Craft and Structure)

3. The War of 1812 is considered a war without a clear winner. Do you agree or disagree? Explain your position with details from this text or others. (Integration of Knowledge and Ideas)

INDEX